DOWNLOADING AND ONLINE SHOPPING
SAFETY AND PRIVACY

j
004.678
Su2d

LASELL COLLEGE LIBRARY
80A Maple St.
Auburndale, MA 02466

ANASTASIA SUEN

rosen publishing's
**rosen
central**

New York

Published in 2014 by The Rosen Publishing Group, Inc.
29 East 21st Street, New York, NY 10010

Copyright © 2014 by The Rosen Publishing Group, Inc.

First Edition

All rights reserved. No part of this book may be reproduced in any form without permission in writing from the publisher, except by a reviewer.

Library of Congress Cataloging-in-Publication Data

Suen, Anastasia.
Downloading and online shopping safety and privacy/Anastasia Suen.—
1st ed.—New York: Rosen, c2014
    p. cm.—(21st century safety and privacy)
Includes bibliographical references and index.
ISBN: 978-1-4488-9571-7 (Library Binding)
ISBN: 978-1-4488-9582-3 (Paperback)
ISBN: 978-1-4488-9583-0 (6-pack)
1. Internet–Security measures–Juvenile literature. 2. Computer security. 3. Computer network resources–Evaluation–Juvenile literature. 4. Money–Juvenile literature. 5. Electronic commerce. I. Title.
TK5105.875.I57 .S84 2014
004.678

Manufactured in the United States of America

CPSIA Compliance Information: Batch #S13YA: For further information, contact Rosen Publishing, New York, New York, at 1-800-237-9932.

CONTENTS

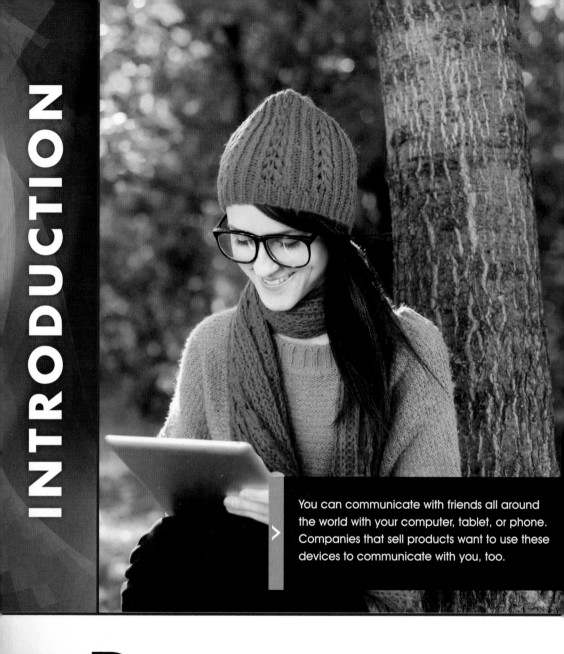

You can communicate with friends all around the world with your computer, tablet, or phone. Companies that sell products want to use these devices to communicate with you, too.

Did you know that many businesses see children and teens as potential consumers? They try to sell things to young people on TV, at the movies, and in fast-food places. Now that so many children are using computers, tablets, and phones, companies have a new way to sell to them.

With just a password and a few numbers, a young person can buy something online. It's so easy to do that the costs can add up very quickly. In 2011, the mobile game *Pet Shop Story* had a promotion and made a million dollars in sales in one day.

Are you a savvy shopper? Do you know how to shop online safely and privately? Just because thieves are trying to steal from you doesn't mean they will succeed. You can protect yourself from online thieves by taking the steps outlined in the following material. Learn how to download safely. Some downloads, like security software that updates automatically, protect your tablet, phone, and computer. That's money well spent.

Find out how you can control who tracks you online and who sends you e-mail, too. You want to be in the know for great deals on your favorite products. But that doesn't mean these companies need to know about everything you do online.

Keep thieves out of your personal e-mail account. Set up a "throwaway" e-mail account for all of your online shopping. Learn what to do if your e-mail is hacked.

Discover how you can shop safely. Buy what you need without paying extra fees. See how the law protects your credit and debit cards.

Thieves steal from children and teens without ever meeting them. It's your numbers that thieves want. If they are stolen, your parents can get them back for you. The law is on your side.

CHAPTER ONE

DOWNLOADS

In May 2012, the game *Angry Birds* reached one billion downloads. This mobile game, one that you play on your phone or tablet, was only three years old. One billion people around the world were trying to help the birds get back at the green pigs for stealing their eggs.

Welcome to the new age of gaming, where free downloads are often the way to play. In 2012, almost 60 percent of children ages eight to eleven years old interviewed by the research firm KidSay used phone apps. That number was just 40 percent the year before.

In the old days, the only way to play a game at home was to purchase a box with software inside and upload it to your computer or gaming console. All of that was when large machines that stayed in one place were all you could buy to play games.

When smaller handheld devices for games were invented, you could take your games with you. The games fit in your pocket or your backpack, but you still had to buy a special device from a gaming company to play.

Today, mobile devices are often where games are played. Now that so many people have cell phones and

4:39 PM

iPod

Today you can play mobile games on your handheld devices, even your phone. Because you can take them anywhere, mobile games, like *Angry Birds*, are very popular.

tablets, game companies want to make money there, too. They have found a way to do that with the "freemium" model. They make their games free to download.

If you don't buy a special gaming device or software, then how do the gaming companies make money? Some free games have ads. The gaming companies get paid to place these ads in their games. Every time you play the game, you see the ads. The ads keep the company names on your mind.

The other way gaming companies make money is by offering upgrades. You can buy a version of the game

> DO THE MATH

A "free" game download can end up costing you a lot more than a game that you buy at the store. If you buy a game for your home gaming console, after you pay $49.99 for the game disc, you can play the game as many times as you want. You don't have to pay again to move up to a new level. Everything you need is already there in the game.

A download may be free, but that might not be the whole picture. If the game asks you to pay $99.99 after just sixty seconds, isn't it really a $99.99 game? Or will it cost you even more? What happens after you use the 100,000 coins in the game? Will you have to stop playing unless you spend more? The costs can add up quickly. If you can't play the game without spending money, that "free" game isn't really free after all.

without ads. Or you can buy items to use in your game. You don't have to do anything special to make that happen. As you play these "free" games, you will see pop-ups asking you to buy what the game says you need. The *Wall Street Journal* reported that after playing the game *Tiny Zoo* for sixty seconds, a message popped up saying, "Looks like you need more Coins to buy Chickity Puff. Purchase 100,000 coins for $99.99."

Too Good to Be True

There are many free downloads today. You can download free apps for your phone or tablet from an app store. You can find free programs for your computer to download online. The only thing is, some of these free downloads aren't really free.

Some "free" downloads are only part of the actual product. To get the entire thing, you have to pay for the rest. This isn't always stated up front, so it may come as a surprise. You often don't find out until after you have downloaded the product and try to use it.

Other free downloads sometimes have a hidden surprise. They give you what they said they would, and a little more. You think you're downloading a free app or program, but that may not be all you're getting. Some hackers add spyware or malware to items they "give away" for free.

What is a hacker? That's what we call a person who breaks in to someone else's computer from far away. A hacker can be on the other side of the world as he breaks in.

Free downloads sometimes let hackers break in to your computer. After you have installed their programs, the hackers, not you, control your computer. Your computer is now a robot, also called a "bot" or a "zombie." It is part of the botnet, the network of remotely controlled computers all over the world.

In 2010, this twenty-three-year-old French man was arrested for hacking. In one of his attacks on the Twitter online social network, he sabotaged the account of U.S. president Barack Obama.

Hackers who add malware to downloads use your computer to send spam or viruses. They may even try to use it to attack other computers. All of this is done through the program that you downloaded. After that, it works automatically.

If a hacker added spyware to a download, he can spy on you. If you type your name, your password, and your numbers into a Web site to buy something, the hacker can see it all. He can steal your identity because he tricked you with a freebie.

> RANSOMWARE

Have you ever seen a TV show or movie where the bad guys held someone for ransom? They kidnap someone and then ask the person's family to send money to let the person go. Hackers do that with downloads. It's called ransomware.

When a ransomware program starts, it holds your computer hostage. A message appears on your computer screen, but nothing else on your computer works. The message says that you have to pay money to set your computer free.

To get you to pay them the money, the hackers try to scare you. One ransomware program says it is from the FBI, the Federal Bureau of Investigation. The hacker wants you to think that the FBI is after you because of your download. The screen says that you have broken the law and that you must pay a fine. They even have the FBI logo there on the screen.

The hackers want you to click on the link and pay them. What you really need to do is to remove the hacker's program from your computer. If you can't do it yourself, you will have to take your computer in for repairs.

Before you download anything, look at the Web site again. Have you ever heard of this company? Does it look real? Hackers can copy art, so the words are your best clue. Big companies hire pros to write their pages. If the words on the page don't sound like what you would hear on TV, it's probably a fake page. Don't download the freebie. Close your browser window and protect yourself instead. Some things really are too good to be true.

Protect Your Device

Hackers are always busy thinking of new ways to steal from you. To keep your devices safe you must use security software. If you own a PC, you can buy the software at the store or go online and download it from a reliable security software company, like Norton or McAfee. The first

Do you ever wonder what it looks like behind the scenes at a security software company? Above, a senior systems lab engineer works on a network server at Norton's company headquarters, Symantec Corporation.

download won't be your last. Your security software will usually last a year. (You can also buy a two- or three-year plan.) Apple computers are sold with security safeguards in place, as long as you run updates when you are prompted.

Security software companies will send you an update each time they discover a new danger. They work full-time to find out what new tricks the hackers are using. Then they create a way to protect your devices from these tricks and send it to you to download.

To keep your devices safe, download each update as soon as it comes. Set up your device to update automatically. Keep your devices safe from hackers.

CHAPTER TWO

TRACKING

Did you know that you are being watched online? As you surf the Web, little strings of code track your every move. Many years ago, theses tracking code were given the name "cookies." The idea was that you could follow the trail of cookie crumbs across the Web to see where a person went.

Remember Hansel and Gretel? In this fairy tale, the children leave a trail of bread crumbs behind them so that they can find their way back home. Unfortunately, the birds eat all of their crumbs and they end up at the witch's house instead. The witch invites them inside, and later she tries to eat them.

Will your time online end like Hansel and Gretel? Will the people who invite you into their homes—their Web sites—try to consume you? Let's look a little closer and see how it works. After all, when you are the one who is shopping, we call you the consumer. You don't want the places where you shop to consume you instead.

In 2012, the computer magazine *PCWorld* reported that Google and Facebook were the top two tracking companies. Each company has multiple ways to follow Web site visitors.

Governments are keeping a close eye on companies, like Facebook, that save their user's personal information. Facebook has been taken to court several times because of its privacy practices.

Google Analytics was at the top of the list. Analytics is a free tool that Google offers to owners of Web sites. After adding Google Analytics code to a Web site, the owner can see how many people came to the Web site. It also tells the owner where viewers came from, which kind of computer they used, and which pages they viewed. It tracks visitors from page to page until they leave the Web site. The final item it reports is how long each visitor was at the Web page.

According to *PCWorld*, there are tens of millions of Web sites around the world using this free tool from

> COPPA

The federal government has laws to protect children online. In 1998, it created COPPA, the Children's Online Privacy Protection Act. This act says that Web sites cannot collect any information about anyone under the age of thirteen without a parent's consent.

Companies that don't follow these rules have to pay big fines. In October 2012, a company that ran fan Web sites for pop stars Justin Bieber, Selena Gomez, Rihanna, and Demi Lovato had to pay a $1 million fine. It had violated COPPA by collecting personal information from 101,000 children (age twelve and under) without their parents' permission. These children had filled out forms on the fan Web sites with their name, home address, e-mail address, phone number, and birth date. The Web page said parent's permission was needed to provide this information. But when permission wasn't given, it saved the children's information anyway, and that is against the law.

Google. These cookies are called first-party cookies. They only leave a trail of where you went at the Web site. They show where you came from and where you went. But they only report on what happened in one place.

If you don't delete these cookies, the Web site will recognize them when you go back. It will log you as a "returning" user. This is how Web sites remember your "preferences." If you are member of a Web site, it will ask you to log in. This is how the Web site knows who you are. After you log in, the Web site can show you the items in your shopping cart. It can show you the new e-mail that came for you. It can remember which online game character you are and how many points you have.

First-party cookies are for only one Web site. They can help you get what you want. They can help you as a Web page user and as a consumer.

Third-party cookies are also found on many Web sites. These are the cookies placed in the ads. Third-party cookies are created by advertisers. They pay to have their ads placed on Web sites that are free to use.

Advertisers who use third-party cookies don't use a single Web site. Advertisers place ads all over the Web. That's their job, to advertise products. They place their ads on free Web sites all over. They do that so that they can see who visits. They are collecting data about you.

When you visit a free site, the code in the ad notices that you are there. It gives your device a third-party cookie. If that company also advertises at the next Web site you visit, the cookie and the advertiser know that you were there. If the third and fourth Web sites you visit also have ads from this company, they have gathered even more information about you.

Just because a company pays for an ad doesn't mean it needs to know where you went online. Why does visiting a Web site give someone else the right to collect information about you? What about your right to privacy?

The Federal Trade Commission

Did you know that the government has an agency to protect you as a consumer? That agency is the FTC, the Federal Trade Commission. Trade is the act of buying and selling. It's another word for shopping. One of the FTC's jobs is to protect consumer privacy. Just because you buy something doesn't mean that the company selling you the item needs to know everything about you.

Companies can stay in business only by selling products or services. Many companies have a sales staff that works with customers. Sales used to be made door to door. A salesperson would come to your house and knock on the door. After you opened the door, the person would try to sell you

You can see the scales of justice on the Federal Trade Commission seal. The FTC is the government agency that protects consumers. It was one of the agencies that took Facebook to court.

something. To stop salespeople from knocking on your door, you needed to put up a "No Soliciting" sign.

When the phone became popular, sales moved there, too. Selling over the phone is called telemarketing. These salespeople don't walk down the street and go door to door. Telemarketers work in a room filled with telephones. They call number after number trying to make a sale. To stop telemarketers from calling you, you can add your phone number to the FTC's Do Not Call Registry. After your phone number has been on the National Do Not Call Registry for thirty-one days, telemarketers are not supposed to call you.

A telemarketer is a person who tries to sell you things over the phone. If you don't want to be called, ask the person to take you off the list.

Do Not Track Me

Nowadays many people buy things online. The FTC is working to protect you here, too. In 2010, the FTC issued a report about a Do Not Track option for the Web. It wants to give you a choice when you shop online. The FTC wants to allow you to choose who can see where you go online. At the present time, companies can follow you online just because you visit their Web page. You have to visit only once to get the tracking started. After a single visit, a tracking cookie is placed on your device. It will stay there until you delete it. And while it is there, it can send information back to the company that placed it there.

There are several things you can do to stop these cookies, but they all require action on your part. The FTC wants to change that. The Do Not Track option reverses the current situation. At the present time it is up to you to stop the cookies from tracking you. The FTC wants to give you control over who can track you first. It suggests doing that in your Web browser. With a single setting, you would be able to stop Web sites from tracking you without your permission.

As you can imagine, advertisers are not in favor of this change. They insist that the reason so much is free online is because they are allowed to track you. You let them track you, so they give you free services. At the present time, this is how many Web sites work. They are free to use because the ads pay their bills. But if an ad on one Web site is on another Web site you visit, that company knows you visited both places. Why do they need to know that? Advertisers argue that it helps them see what you like so that they can sell you the "right" products. They say it will help you, and it might, but do you always have to be "on" when you are online? Do you always have to be under the spotlight? Can't you live your life without ad companies watching you 24/7?

MYTHS AND FACTS

Myth: Free downloads save me money.

Fact: Some free downloads aren't really free. If a download also gives your phone or computer a virus, it can cost you both time and money to fix.

Myth: No one can see what I look at when I shop on my computer, tablet, or phone.

Fact: Each shopping Web site you visit places a small file, called a cookie, on your device. Companies use these cookies to track your movements online so that they can see what interests you.

Myth: My credit and debit cards are safe when I shop online.

Fact: A stranger can add spyware to your device by giving you a free download. That spyware will let him see what you write on a Web page form. That includes your debit and credit card numbers.

CHAPTER THREE

SAFE E-MAIL

One of the dangers of downloading is having your computer taken over by hackers. If the download also has malware in it, your computer will be turned into a bot. Hackers can use it to send spam. Spam is the name of a canned meat, but the word is also used another way. Spam is the word we use for unwanted e-mail.

Unwanted E-mail

In a perfect world, you would get e-mail only from the people you knew. But for many people, there is always something more in their e-mail in-boxes. They get e-mails asking them to buy things.

Companies are always trying to sell you something, and many use e-mail to do that. They do it because it works. After every mailing, some people click on the ads and buy things. Not everyone does that, of course, but that's how sales work. Not everyone who goes to a store in person or online buys everything they see. Sales are a numbers game. If companies can make enough to pay their bills and have some money left over, they can stay in business.

Don't let spoofers and hackers take over your e-mail. Report it instead! Forward the unwanted mail to your e-mail provider. It knows how to stop it.

The number they have to meet is known only to them. Your job, as they see it, is to read the ad and buy!

Of course, you and your parents have your own numbers to worry about. If you want to buy something that costs more than you have, you will have to wait a while. You will have to save up to buy what you want or what you need.

If you sign up for news from your favorite store, its ads aren't spam to you. If you change your mind, you can stop these e-mails. Just go to the bottom of the e-mail and click on the word "Unsubscribe." Then the e-mails will stop. That's what reputable businesses do. They respect your rights as a consumer. They follow the law.

> SPOOFERS

Have you ever had a message come to you from your own e-mail address? If you didn't send it to yourself, then you have been spoofed. A spammer is using a computer program called a bot. This spoofing program writes the To: address (that's you) in the From: address line. If you report this e-mail as spam, the tech people can figure out who really sent it and block him. Just to be safe, change your password.

The e-mails you need to worry about are the kind that won't let you unsubscribe. A hacker isn't worried about your rights as a consumer. A hacker isn't following the law. No, what a hacker wants is to take over your computer, and steal your identity and your cash. To do that, a hacker wants you to click on the link in the spam he sent. It's not a link that lets you unsubscribe. This link will download a program into your computer that will let him take control.

E-mail Hacks

Did you know that e-mail can be hacked, too? During the 2012 presidential campaign, a hacker claimed that he broke into one of the candidates' e-mail accounts. Mitt

Romney was one of many people hacked that summer. But Romney's hacker did something that most don't. Romney's hacker bragged about it to the reporters at *Gawker*, an online news and gossip Web site. The hacker didn't want to tell the reporters his name, but he did want everyone to know what he had done. He sent the reporters an e-mail with a new password for Romney's private Hotmail address. The hacker invited the reporters to check it for themselves. The reporters didn't do that. It's against the law to read

With mobile devices, you can work anywhere. Mitt Romney, the former governor of Massachusetts, ran for president in 2012. After a stop in Iowa, he worked at his computer on the campaign bus.

someone else's e-mail. What they did instead was report that the hacker had contacted them.

The Romney hacker used the e-mail system itself to break in. When Romney was the governor of Massachusetts, he used his Hotmail address for some of his government work. This personal Hotmail address was mentioned in the news, so everyone knew what it was. After it went public, the hacker attacked.

If you know your e-mail address but have forgotten the password, you can use the password recovery tool. The hacker told the reporters that he was able to log in because he guessed the name of Romney's pet. The name of your favorite pet is a common security question. Because Romney was a public figure, the name of his pets had also been reported in the newspaper. After the hacker guessed the pet's name, he logged in and reset the password.

Has Your E-mail Been Hacked?

You don't have to be famous to get hacked. E-mail hacking can happen to anyone, even you and your friends. If a hacker has changed your password, then you won't be able to log in. But that's not the only thing hackers do.

How else do you know if your e-mail has been hacked? Do you suddenly have a lot of mailer-daemon messages? Those are e-mails telling you that your message was rejected. But you know that you didn't send those rejected messages in the first place.

Are your friends telling you that they are getting strange e-mails from you? The e-mails look like they come from your e-mail address, but you know you didn't send them.

Has anything in your e-mail changed? Are things missing or have new items been added? Look at all of the folders in your e-mail. Are messages there that you didn't write? Or have all of the messages in your e-mail folders been erased? Have the e-mail addresses in your address book been deleted? Or have new addresses been added? Some hackers add things while others subtract them.

What to Do When Your E-mail Has Been Hacked

If you think that your e-mail has been hacked, the first thing to do is check your online security. The most common way for hackers to find out your passwords is from inside your own computer! If you change your passwords without updating your security software, you haven't kicked out the hacker. The hacker can still get to anything you have in your computer, even the new passwords. So run the security software first, and let it clean up the mess. It should get rid of the viruses or malware that the hacker used to get access to your computer. You didn't see it come in, but a page you opened or a program you downloaded had something attached to it. Once the "bug" was installed in your computer, it gave the hacker access.

> The Department of Homeland Security also looks for cyber crime. It shares information about cyber threats and system vulnerabilities with other government agencies. This cyber security analyst works at the Malware Laboratory in Idaho.

After you clean your computer, sign in to your e-mail and change your password. Now you are safe from the hacker. He isn't in your computer anymore, and he doesn't know your new password.

If you can't sign in to your e-mail, contact the e-mail server and let it know. It will know how to help you get your e-mail back. Some companies even save your deleted messages for a short time so that you can restore them after a hacker attacks. This is why your e-mail trash does not always disappear right away.

Use a Throwaway E-mail Account

To stay ahead of hackers, experts recommend creating a throwaway e-mail account. This is an e-mail address that you use only for shopping online. None of your private e-mails will be in this account. It is only for things you do online.

Use one of the free e-mail services online for your throwaway e-mail. Hotmail, Yahoo! Mail, and Gmail are all free. Anyone who goes online can set up an e-mail account with one of these services. The reason is that the free e-mail companies want you to visit their pages often so that you can see their ads.

Why do you need an e-mail account that you can "throw away?" If one of the stores you shop with online has its data stolen, that means your data is stolen, too. The credit card company has steps in place to protect your credit. It can stop any credit card purchases made with stolen numbers. It can close your account and give you a completely new number.

If you have an e-mail account just for shopping, you can do the same. If your data is stolen, you can close that account and start a new one. None of your personal e-mails will be lost because they are in another private e-mail account. Using an e-mail address just for shopping can protect you online.

Going Phishing

When you shop online, stores want to keep in touch with you. They want you to shop there again, so most online merchants ask you to sign up for their e-mails. They promise to send you news about sales and new products. They want you to know when your favorite thing comes into the store so that you can buy it from them. You want to know about it, too, so you decide to sign up. The e-mails go directly to your throwaway e-mail account. Now you know the latest about your favorite items at your favorite store. All is well...until you get an e-mail that asks you to check your password. It tells you that something has gone terribly wrong and you need to log on right now and fix it. Just click this link and you can take care of it right away.

You have just met a phisher. The e-mail that came to you wasn't from the store. A store doesn't need you to check your password. The store already knows what it is. That e-mail came from one who was "fishing" for information. A phisher (say it like "fisher") is someone who wants to steal your identity. This thief wants your passwords, and better yet, he wants your credit card information, too.

Some online sites allow you to save your credit card information. Your password and your credit card information are linked. When someone steals your password, he is hoping he can steal your credit card information, too. While you are busy living your life, the thief is busy trying to steal from you.

Don't Take the Bait

How can you protect yourself? Don't take the bait. If you get an e-mail asking you to log in and fix something, don't do it. The store didn't send that message. Neither did its "IT Department." Stores send e-mails filled with photos of things to buy. Stores send e-mails with sales coupons and great deals that expire if you don't hurry and buy now. The store is focused on the merchandise, not your password.

A phisher, on the other hand, is all about the password. He wants your log-in name and your password, too. He has gone to great lengths to try and trick you. He wants your credit card numbers so that he can buy what he wants… with your money.

CHAPTER FOUR

SAFE SHOPPING

Advertisers really want your business. They want to know who you are and what you look at online. To do that, they advertise on popular Web pages. That allows them to collect data about many users quickly.

Selling Your Information

The amount of information that advertisers collect about you is increasing. In November 2010, a visit to a popular Web site would trigger ten "instances of data-collection." In December 2011, it was up to fifty-six, according to data-management company Krux Digital Inc.

What makes this data so important? The *Wall Street Journal* reported that online advertisers conduct ad auctions. At these auctions, they sell your search information to the highest bidder. Advertisers sell the information they have already gathered about you and where you are looking now. The auction takes place in real time. That means they sell your data as soon as you visit a Web page. While you are looking at the items on a Web page, somewhere a computer may be calculating the price of your

After a hacker broke into its computer network, Zappos notified all of its customers. The company told them to reset their passwords. It invalidated the old passwords so that the hacker couldn't use them.

information. Other computers are deciding if they want to buy it, and a sale is made.

Computer algorithms make it all happen. That's how the stock market works now. The computer is given a set of instructions to follow. It can follow those instructions "hundreds of times every second," says physicist Sean Gourley. He goes on to say that the human mind can make a decision in "about 650 milliseconds or about .65 of the second." An algorithm, on the other hand, "can trade on the order of microseconds or millionths of a second."

Before You Use Mom's Credit Card

Did you know that some advertisers that track you on the Web can also see what you fill out on that Web page? Yes, they can see what you write on the Web pages that they track. This is why it is so important to make sure that a page is secure before you use mom or dad's credit card. You don't want to give your parents' credit card numbers away! Strangers could use the numbers to buy things for themselves or they could sell the numbers to someone else.

How do you know that a page is secure? Look for the lock at the top of the page. A secure Web page has a small yellow lock at the top that closes when it is secure. The address also changes from "http" to "https." The extra "s" stands for "secure." Some pages also turn green at the top when the https and the lock appear.

If a Web page offers you the option to buy something and a lock does not appear, don't use your credit card. You might be at a fake Web page. Some thieves make Web pages that look just like the real thing. These fakes are so close that it looks like you are at the store's Web page when you're not.

How can you tell if a shopping Web site is real or just a fake? After you click on the "Add to Cart" button, go to your shopping cart and look at the top of the page. If the lock does not appear automatically, your credit card information is not secure. If you type your credit card numbers

> DEBIT CARD OR
> CREDIT CARD?

Your parents may allow you to shop with a debit card. When you use a debit card, it takes money out of a checking account to pay for your purchases. Debit cards can be very helpful. When you use a debit card, you pay for the item right away. You won't get a bill later.

The problem comes when a debit card is stolen. The card takes money out of your bank account. A thief can use your debit card numbers to empty your bank account. The money goes out and it doesn't come back.

When you use a credit card, you don't pay the bill until later. Credit card companies pay the bill first, so they are very careful. If it appears that someone may have stolen your credit card numbers, a credit card company will stop all payments. You do not have to pay for the stolen items. The company will give you a new credit card with new numbers. The old numbers won't work anymore. The stealing stops. If you suspect that someone may be using your credit card information, call your credit card company immediately.

in the form on that page, your numbers can be stolen. Close the page and clean your cache right away. Go to your Web browser history and delete all of the pages you have visited. That will remove the page from your history and delete all of the cookies that might have been added.

Shopping with Your Smartphone

If you are shopping with your smartphone, the same rules apply. If a lock doesn't appear on the page, don't buy anything there. The lock needs to show or you just can't trust it. You need to protect your phone just like you protect your computer. Your computer has lots of e-mail addresses that can be hacked, but your phone has phone numbers that can be stolen. It may also have home addresses, too. All of that data is valuable to a hacker. He doesn't care about you; he only wants what he can steal.

Reporting Stolen Numbers

Your credit or debit card numbers can be stolen from your computer or your smartphone without your knowledge. Thieves can use your card numbers even if you still have the card in your wallet. The only way to find out if your numbers were stolen is to check your account. You need to log in and see what is on the bill.

You can download apps onto your phone to help you shop. Shopping apps can help you find stores near you or compare prices. Some are just for coupons, so you can save money.

Most teens don't pay their own bills, so they don't ever check the bill for fraud. Unfortunately, after they get their own cards, many young adults continue this practice. In the 2009 Identity Fraud Survey Report, young adults eighteen to twenty-four years old took on average 132 days to discovery that their identity had been stolen. That's more than four months! This is much longer than the twenty-nine days that adults sixty-five years and older took to find out.

Why does it matter? The longer it takes to discover identity theft, the more money you can lose. Every day that thieves have your card numbers is a day that they can use those numbers to steal from you. They can charge items on your credit card or use your debit card to empty out your bank account.

The Law Protects You

There are laws that protect you from losses due to fraud. Credit cards are protected by the Fair Credit Billing Act (FCBA). The FCBA says that if your credit card is stolen, you are responsible for only $50. If the numbers were stolen but you still have the card, you are not responsible for any charges. You don't have to pay a penny of what was charged with your credit card numbers. Don't pay your credit card bill without checking to see what was charged. You don't want to pay for things you didn't buy.

Debit cards are protected by the Electronic Fund Transfer Act (EFTA). How quickly you report the theft determines

Make it a habit to check your monthly bank and credit card statements. If you see charges you didn't make, contact the bank or the credit card company right away.

what you have to pay. If you discover that your card was stolen and report it right away, you may not lose any money. But that changes as the days go by. The longer it takes you to find the losses, the more money you can lose from your bank account. If you have overdraft protection on your account, the costs can really add up. The bank will allow the thieves to withdraw more money than you have and will charge you a fee each time it happens. You could end up owing the bank more money than you had in your account!

The best way to stop fraud is to check on your cards regularly. When you have your own cards, keep your money safe. Log in once a week and see if what the bank statement says matches what you bought. Sign up for bank alerts. The bank will e-mail or text you when your balance is too low. Then you can log in and see what's going on. Check your credit card statement, too, while you are online and keep your money safe. You worked hard to earn it. Don't let anyone take it from you.

CHAPTER FIVE

IDENTITY THEFT

Carter Andrushko, a five-year-old boy in Utah, has been working since before he was born. Well, not really, but that's what his numbers say. You see, when a person is born in the United States, he or she is assigned a number—a Social Security number. This number is assigned by the Social Security Administration, a part of the federal government. When you grow up, you need this number to prove your identity.

You probably have a Social Security number, too. It is given to you free of charge when you are born. Your parents sent in your birth certificate, and a few weeks later, your card came. The numbers on your card are only for you, no one else. When someone else used Carter's numbers, they stole his identity.

Necessary Numbers

Whenever you start a new job, you must fill out two forms, a W-4 and an I-9. Both of these forms are required by the federal government. On the W-4, you sign up to be taxed at a certain rate. The tax pays for the government services that we all use.

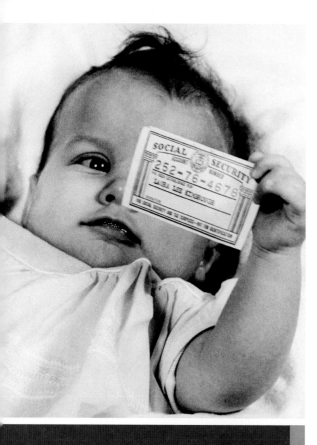

In the United States, every new baby is given a Social Security number. This number is used to buy financial gifts for the infant, like stocks and bonds. Later it is used for employment.

An I-9 form certifies that you are eligible to be employed in this country. If you aren't eligible, employers are not supposed to hire you. Employers must keep an I-9 file for every employee they have. They have to save the files for three years.

So what does this have to do with downloading and shopping online? You need the number on your Social Security card to fill out both the W-4 and I-9 forms. That makes this number very valuable. It's a number that thieves online want to steal.

Stolen Numbers

Sometimes immigrants who are not U.S. citizens buy stolen Social Security numbers so that they can get a job. The company they work for doesn't know that the numbers really belong to a child. The company sends in the money it collects from each paycheck. It sends it in for taxes (the W-4) and for Social Security payments (the I-9). If a child isn't using those numbers at the time, no one is the wiser.

Criminals use stolen numbers to buy things for themselves. When it is time to pay for these items, these criminals don't pay the bill. But they don't care. They didn't use their real names. The crooks used the names and numbers of someone else.

In 2012, Carnegie Mellon University's CyLab found 10.2 percent of the forty-three thousand children it studied through background checks had their identity stolen. That may seem like a small number, but it's fifty-one times the rate of identity theft for adults.

Most families don't check their children's numbers, so thieves can use them for years. Now that more and more records are online, hackers can steal a child's numbers more easily. According to CyLab, hackers even break into computers at schools and medical clinics.

When You Grow Up

If a thief has used your Social Security number for years, what happens later? Unfortunately, when you grow up, the bill collectors want you to pay up. You didn't buy the fancy boat or that expensive car, but someone using your numbers may have, and he didn't pay the bills. Before you get a chance to buy things on your own, your credit rating is ruined.

Unpaid bills are sent to debt collectors. You don't want the debt collectors to come after you for items you didn't buy! Check your credit rating to see if someone else used your numbers.

With a bad credit rating, you can't renew your driver's license. You can't open your own bank account. You can't get a job. The bill collectors want you to pay, but without a car, a bank account, or a job, how can you do that?

Rating Credit

There are three companies that give credit ratings: Equifax, Experian, and TransUnion. Each company looks at what you buy and how you pay. They use your shopping and

> ASK FOR A CREDIT CHECK
> FOR YOUR SIXTEENTH BIRTHDAY

You don't have to wait until you grow up to see if your numbers were stolen. Ask your parents for a credit check for your sixteenth birthday. If you have had your identity stolen, that gives your parents time to clean things up before you need to use your credit rating by yourself. Then you won't have to pay the price later. You won't be responsible for someone else's bills. You will only have to pay for what you buy.

Making sure that you have a good credit record when you become an adult is very important. You want to be able to renew your driver's license. You want to have your own bank account. You need to get a job to make a living for yourself. If you have a bad credit record, employers won't hire you. The FTC recommends that your parents ask for a "manual search based on the child's Social Security number." That allows the credit agencies to see if your number has been used by anyone else.

payment history to create a credit score for you. This score is your credit rating.

Your credit rating determines what you can do with your credit card as time goes on. If you buy things with a credit card and don't pay the bills, you will end up with a low rating. If you pay your bill each month, you will be given a high rating. The higher your credit rating is, the more you can buy. Companies don't want to take chances with people who don't pay their bills.

The Law Protects You

Your parents can sign up for monthly credit reports for a fee. Each credit agency can send you a copy of your credit scores from all three agencies. A law takes it one step further. The Fair Credit Reporting Act (FCRA) says that each of these companies must give you a free copy of your credit report once every twelve months. They will only send it if you ask, but once you do, the law requires them to send it.

To get a free copy, you need to go online. The free copies come only from a Web site that the companies created together. Your parents can also request it by mail or by phone, but the online version is instant. You see the report right away. The mail and phone options take fifteen days to process.

Each credit agency uses a different formula to create its credit scores. This means that one person can have three different credit scores. The law says that these agencies have to show you the credit score they have given you every twelve months. It doesn't say that your parents have to look at all three reports at the same time. Some families check only one at a time. That way they can keep an eye out for fraud three times a year.

Speaking of fraud, there is only one Web site that gives you a free credit report. But that hasn't stopped others from creating Web pages that say they were free, too. Some charge a fee, while others just steal your numbers. Don't write your Social Security number or your credit card numbers online until you are sure you are at the real Web site.

How to Get Your Identity Back

If your parents discover that someone has stolen your identity, they will have to take action right away. They will need to:

1. Alert each credit reporting agency.
2. Place a fraud alert.
3. Request a credit freeze.
4. File a report with the FTC.
5. File a police report.
6. Call every company with a fraudulent account in your name.

You may need to get a new Social Security number. Of course, this new number will have to be checked as well. And your parents will still have to watch your old number. Some of your records will still use your old number, so having two numbers can get quite complicated.

Protect Your Passwords

There are many things you can do right now to protect yourself from identity theft. Your online passwords are the first place to start. Never ever use your Social Security number as your password. Now that you know how important it is to thieves, it is up to you to keep it private. Never using it online is the best policy.

Creating a strong password is the next step. A longer password, one with eight characters, is best. Mix it up and use numbers and letters. Make some of the letters capitals and keep the others small. Add a symbol or two to make it really hard to guess. Most password programs allow you

Protect yourself! Use a different password for each place you visit online. Otherwise, a hack in one place can put your other accounts in danger, too.

to use the symbols on the number keys of your keyboard. Test it out and see what works. (If a Web page won't accept a symbol, the program it is using will let you know.)

Password protection step number three is to use a different password for each log in. Many Web sites allow you to use a common log-in. These shared password sites allow you to log in to their Web site with your Facebook, Google, or Twitter log-in. It's easier for you to remember just a few passwords, but that means it's also easier for the thieves. Using a different password for each Web site or service makes it harder for the hackers to steal from you.

Changing your passwords regularly is the final step to take. If you change your passwords often, you keep yourself one step ahead of the hackers. Changing your password is the first step you need to take when your smartphone or computer is hacked. Then the old password is useless. Only the new password can open the door. When you change your password, you lock out the hacker. You make his stolen information invalid.

10 GREAT QUESTIONS
TO ASK TECH SUPPORT

Now that you know how many ways there are to steal your identity, find out what settings you need to keep your phone and computer safe. Each make and model has different instructions.

 1 How do I clear the cache on my phone?

 2 How do I clear the history on my phone?

 3 How do I take cookies off my phone?

 4 How do I turn off tracking on my phone?

 5 How do I reset my phone's password?

 6 How do I clear the cache on my computer?

 7 How do I clear the history on my computer?

 8 How do I take cookies off my computer?

 9 How do I turn off tracking on my computer?

 10 How do I reset my Internet browser?

algorithm A set of rules for solving a problem.

app An application; a small, specialized program downloaded onto a computer or mobile device.

auction A public sale where property or goods are sold to whoever pays the most.

bot A program that works by itself; a short form of the word "robot."

browser A program that allows users to find and read files on the World Wide Web.

cache An area of computer memory that saves frequently used or requested data.

cartridge A small removable unit of computer software.

cookie A message with information about a user on the Internet sent back to the person who created the message.

data Facts or pieces of information used by a computer program.

download To copy or transfer (data or a program) from one computer to another.

fraud The act of deceit or trickery for profit or to gain an unfair advantage.

freemium A sales strategy where the basic product or service is free but customers are charged for additional features and content.

hack To break into a computer from a remote location to steal or damage data.

mailer daemon An automated reply sent when an e-mail message cannot be delivered.

malware Software intended to damage a computer or take partial control over its operation.

phisher A person who sends e-mails with fake links to steal financial information from Internet users.

software The programs that tell a computer what to do.

spam Messages sent to e-mail addresses or mobile phones without permission.

spoof To communicate electronically under a false identity.

spyware Software installed without the owner's permission that gathers information about the user and sends it to someone else.

virus A piece of computer code that makes new copies of itself to damage or shut down a system or network.

Annual Credit Report Request Service
P.O. Box 105283
Atlanta, GA 30348-5283
Web site: https://www.annualcreditreport.com/cra/index.jsp
To comply with the Fair Credit Reporting Act,
AnnualCreditReport.com provides consumers with a
free credit report once every twelve months from each
of the three nationwide consumer credit reporting
companies.

Equifax
P.O. Box 740241
Atlanta, GA 30374-0241
(800) 797-6801
Web site: http://www.equifax.com
Equifax is a credit reporting company in twelve countries.

Experian
P.O. Box 9556
Allen, TX 75013
(888) 397-3742
Web site: http://www.experian.com
Experian is a credit reporting company in thirty-six countries.

Federal Bureau of Investigation (FBI)
FBI Headquarters

935 Pennsylvania Avenue NW
Washington, DC 20535-0001
(202) 324-3000
Web site: http://www.fbi.gov
The Federal Bureau of Investigation conducts law
    enforcement operations for the entire nation.

Federal Communications Commission (FCC)
Consumer & Governmental Affairs Bureau
Consumer Inquiries and Complaints Division
445 12th Street SW
Washington, DC 20554
(888) 225-5322
Web site: http://www.fcc.gov/guides/
    spam-unwanted-text-messages-and-email
The Federal Communications Commission enforces the
    CAN-SPAM Act, a law that prohibits e-mail and
    phone spam.

Federal Trade Commission (FTC)
600 Pennsylvania Avenue NW
Washington, DC 20580
(202) 326-2222
Web site: http://www.ftc.gov
The Federal Trade Commission manages
    OnGuardOnline.gov, a Web site that helps you
    avoid scams and keep your computer secure.

Internet Crime Complaint Center (IC3)
National White Collar Crime Center
10900 Nuckols Road, Suite 325
Glen Allen, VA 23060
(800) 221-4424
Web site: http://www.ic3.gov
IC3 is cosponsored by the Federal Bureau of Investigation
and the National White Collar Crime Center (NW3C).

TransUnion
Trans Union Consumer Relations
P.O. Box 2000
Chester, PA 19022-2000
(800) 797-6801
Web site: http://www.transunion.com
TransUnion is a credit reporting company in twenty-nine
countries.

Web Sites

Due to the changing nature of Internet links, Rosen Publishing has developed an online list of Web sites related to the subject of this book. This site is updated regularly. Please use this link to access the list:

http://www.rosenlinks.com/21C/Shop

Bingham, Jane. *Internet Freedom: Where Is the Limit?* Chicago, IL: Heinemann Library, 2007.

Bostick, Nan. *Managing Money.* Costa Mesa, CA: Saddleback Educational Publishing, 2012.

Butler, Tamsen. *The Complete Guide to Personal Finance: For Teenagers.* Ocala, FL: Atlantic Publishing Group, 2010.

Byers, Ann. *First Credit Cards and Credit Smarts.* New York, NY: Rosen Publishing Group, 2010.

Chatzky, Jean. *Not Your Parents' Money Book: Making, Saving, and Spending Your Own Money.* New York, NY: Simon & Schuster Books for Young Readers, 2010.

Cornwall, Phyllis. *Online Etiquette and Safety: Super Smart Information Strategies.* Ann Arbor, MI: Cherry Lake Publishing, 2010.

Fisk, Nathan W. *Understanding Online Piracy: The Truth About Illegal File Sharing.* Santa Barbara, CA: ABC-CLIO, 2009.

Freedman, Jeri. *First Bank Account and First Investments Smarts.* New York, NY: Rosen Publishing Group, 2010.

Gerber, Larry. *Top 10 Tips for Developing Money Management Skills.* New York, NY: Rosen Publishing Group, 2013.

Houghton, Gillian. *How Credit Cards Work.* New York, NY: Rosen Publishing Group, 2009.

Kiyosaki, Robert T. *Rich Dad Poor Dad for Teens: The Secrets About Money—That You Don't Learn in School!* Scottsdale, AZ: Plata Publishing, 2012.

Levete, Sarah. *Taking Action Against Internet Crime.* New York, NY: Rosen Publishing Group, 2010.

Mooney, Carla. *Online Security.* San Diego, CA: Referencepoint Press, 2011.

Orr, Tamra. *Privacy and Hacking.* New York, NY: Rosen Publishing Group, 2008.

Peterson, Judy Monroe. *First Budget Smarts.* New York, NY: Rosen Publishing Group, 2010.

Silver, Don. *High School Money Book.* Los Angeles, CA: Adams-Hall Publishing, 2008.

Simons, Rae. *Spending Money. Broomall*, PA: Mason Crest Publishers, 2010.

Swanson, Jennifer. *How the Internet Works.* North Mankato, MN: The Childs World, 2011.

Thompson, Helen. *Understanding Credit.* Broomall, PA: Mason Crest Publishers, 2011.

AOL. "How Do I Know If My Account Has Been
    Compromised (Hacked)?" Retrieved June 15, 2012
    (http://help.aol.com/help/microsites/search.do?cm
    d=displayKC&externalId=51598).
Dixon, Pam. "Consumer Tips: How to Opt-Out of Cookies
    That Track You." World Privacy Forum, March 2011.
    Retrieved September 18, 2012 (http://www.world
    privacyforum.org/cookieoptout.html).
Federal Trade Commission. "Children's Online Privacy
    Protection Act of 1998." 1998. Retrieved April 8, 2012
    (http://www.ftc.gov/ogc/coppa1.htm).
Federal Trade Commission. "Your Access to Free Credit
    Reports." November 2, 2011. Retrieved September 28,
    2012 (www.ftc.gov/bcp/edu/pubs/consumer/credit/
    cre34.shtm).
Hotmail Help & How-to. "Hacked Account." Windows,
    February 23, 2012. Retrieved June 17, 2012 (http://
    windows.microsoft.com/is-IS/hotmail/hacked
    -account-faq).
Liebowitz, Matt. "Did Someone Hack Mitt Romney's Hotmail
    Account?" NBC News, June 5, 2012. Retrieved June
    14, 2012 (http://www.nbcnews.com/technology/
    technolog/did-someone-hack-mitt-romneys-hotmail
    -account-815270).
McCullagh, Declan. "FTC Wants Voluntary 'Do Not Track'
    for the Web." CNET, December 1, 2010. Retrieved June

19, 2012 (http://news.cnet.com/8301-13578_3-20024332-38.html).

Microsoft Corporation. "How to Use Tracking Protection and ActiveX Filtering in Internet Explorer 9." Windows, 2012. Retrieved June 17, 2012 (http://windows.microsoft .com/en-US/windows7/How-to-use-Tracking-Protection -and-ActiveX-Filtering).

Microsoft Support. "Computer Viruses: Description, Prevention, and Recovery." March 2, 2012. Retrieved April 8, 2012 (http://support.microsoft.com/kb/129972).

Mills. Eleanor. "Romney Pet Plays Part in Alleged E-mail Hack." CNET, June 5, 2012. Retrieved June 14, 2012 (http://news.cnet.com/8301-1009_3-57447944-83/romney-pet-plays-part-in-alleged-e-mail-hack).

Molina, Brett. "'Angry Birds' tops 1 Billion Downloads." *USA Today*, May 9, 2012. Retrieved October 3, 2012 (http: //content.usatoday.com/communities/gamehunters/ post/2012/05/angry-birds-tops-1-billion-downloads/ 1%E2%80%A6#.UHMaaJhZXvE).

National Public Radio. "In Wall Street 2.0, Computers Are King." August 18, 2012. Retrieved October 5, 2012 (http://www.npr.org/2012/08/18/159082822/ in-wall-street-2-0-computers-are-king).

Norton. "Bots and Botnets — A Growing Threat." Retrieved September 26, 2012 (http://us.norton .com/botnet/promo).

Pan, Joann. "Rovio Rejoices Over Billionth Angry Birds Download." Mashable.com, May 9, 2012. Retrieved October 3, 2012 (http://mashable.com/2012/05/09/angry-birds-1-billion-downloads).

Richmond, Riva. "A Seven-Step Guide to Protecting Customer Privacy." Entrepreneur.com, January 5, 2012. Retrieved June 15, 2012 (http://www.entrepreneur.com/article/222552).

Simon, Jeremy M. "Young Adults Slow to Spot ID Theft, Survey Shows." Creditcards.com, February 10, 2010. Retrieved June 20, 2012 (http://www.creditcards.com/credit-card-news/javelin-identity-theft-survey-09-1276.php).

Singer, Natasha. "Fan Sites Settle Children's Privacy Charges." *New York Times*, October 3, 2012. Retrieved October 4, 2012 (http://www.nytimes.com/2012/10/04/technology/fan-sites-for-pop-stars-settle-childrens-privacy-charges.html).

Troianovski, Anton, Spencer E. Ante, and Jessica E. Vascellaro. "Mom, Please Feed My Apps!" *Wall Street Journal*, June 9, 2012. Retrieved June 11, 2012 (http://online.wsj.com/article/SB10001424052702303753904577452341745766920.html).

Tynan, Dan. "Facebook, Google Top List of Firms Tracking You Online, Report." *PCWorld*, June 14, 2012. Retrieved June 14, 2012 (http://www.pcworld.com/article/257603/facebook_google_top_list_of_firms_tracking_you_online_report.html).

T

tech support, questions to ask, 50
telemarketing, 19
third-party cookies, 17
Tiny Zoo, 8
tracking, 5, 14–21, 22, 35
   protections against, 20–21
Twitter, 49

V

viruses, 10, 22, 28

W

Web sites
   ads on, 17, 21, 33
   fake, 35
   secure, 35
W-4 forms, 41, 43

Y

Yahoo! Mail, 30

About the Author

Anastasia Suen is the author of more than 150 books for children and adults. She has taught kindergarten to college, and has worked as a children's literature consultant for many years. The daughter of an engineer, she has taught online since 2000 and helped many students learn how to work safely on the Web. Suen lives with her family in Plano, Texas.

Photo Credits

Cover (figure with laptop) East/Shutterstock.com; cover (background) Annette Shaff/Shutterstock.com; p. 4 Martin Dimitrov/E+/Getty Images; p. 7 Justin Sullivan/Getty Images; p. 10 Thierry Zoccolan/AFP/Getty Images; p. 12 Bloomberg/Getty Images; pp. 15, 18, 26, 29, 37, 42 © AP Images; p. 19 Jupiterimages/Pixland/Thinkstock; p. 24 Ana Blazic Pavlovic/Shutterstock.com; p. 34 Karen Bleier/AFP/Getty Images; p. 39 Digital Vision/Getty Images; p. 44 The Washington Post/Getty Images; p. 48 Press Association via AP Images.

Designer: Michael Moy; Editor: Bethany Bryan; Photo Researcher: Marty Levick